ON WORK

Money, Meaning, Identity

DEREK THOMPSON

zando
NEW YORK

ON WORK by Derek Thompson

Copyright © 2023 by The Atlantic Monthly Group
Introduction copyright © 2023 by Derek Thompson

Page 85 is a continuation of this copyright page.

Zando
zandoprojects.com

First Edition: April 2023

Text and cover design by Oliver Munday

The publisher does not have control over and is not responsible for
author or other third-party websites (or their content).

Library of Congress Control Number: 2022946767

978-1-63893-072-3 (Paperback)
978-1-63893-073-0 (ebook)

10 9 8 7 6 5 4 3 2 1
Manufactured in the United States of America

CONTENTS

INTRODUCTION

HERE IS THE HISTORY OF work in six words: from *jobs*, to *careers*, to *callings*.

For most of human history, there has been little concept of "progress" in our labor. Around the world, people performed similar routine tasks as their parents and their grandparents across the centuries. They harvested wheat. They hammered nails. They assembled gears and sewed thread and patched homes. Their work was a matter of subsistence and necessity. It was not a race for status, or an existential search for meaning. These were jobs, and they still are. For hundreds of millions of people in the US and around the world, *work is work*—grueling, or boring, or exploited, or poorly paid, or all of the above.

In the 19th century, the railroads and the telegraph forced American companies to change the way they organized their labor. In 1800, traveling from Manhattan to Chicago took, on average, four weeks. In 1857, it took two days. As goods and information moved faster than ever, firms headquartered in major cities had to track prices from Los Angeles to Miami. To conduct this full orchestra of operations, they built a new system of organizing labor. They needed managers. "As late as 1840, there were no middle managers in the United States," Alfred Chandler observed in *The Visible Hand*, his classic history of the rise of America's managerial revolution. Rail and telegraphs made new kinds of businesses possible, including department stores, mail-order houses, and the national oil and steel behemoths.

The rise of managers brought on the rise of the professional class—blue-collar, white-collar, every-collar. Large companies required massive, multi-level bureaucracies. And within these laborious labyrinths, workers could ascend from grunt, to manager, to executive. These corporations invented the modern journey of a *career*, that narrative arc bending toward a set of precious initials, like VP, SVP, and CEO.

As the managerial revolution created a sense of professional progress, the decline of organized religion and social integration in the 20th century left many Americans bereft of any sense of spiritual progress in their lives. For some, work rose to fill the void. Many people today ask their jobs to provide community, transcendence, meaning, self-actualization, existential therapy—all the things we have historically sought from organized religion. These workers—particularly, highly educated workers in the white-collar economy—feel that their jobs cannot be "just jobs" and that their careers cannot be "just careers." Their jobs must be their *callings*.

A

Some people simply love their jobs. But many of them are also adherents to a cult of productivity and achievement, where anything short of finding one's vocational soul mate amounts to a wasted life. In a 2019 Pew Research survey, half of Americans said that the most important part of a fulfilling life was work that provided joy and meaning. Just 20 percent said the same about marriage or having children. These workers have founded a kind of new religion in America and around the world that places upon the altar of life the virtues of work, career, achievement. And it's making us a little bit crazy.

I call that new religion "workism." Workism is three things. First, it is the belief that, in a time when religion is in decline, more people, especially the elite, are turning to work to provide everything we have historically expected of organized religions. Second, it is the irony that, in a time of declining trust in most institutions like politics and religion, we expect more than ever from the companies that employ us; and that, in an age of declining community attachments, the workplace has, for many, become the last community standing. Third, it is a mixed blessing. The gospel of labor creates devoted workers and extraordinary achievements, giving purpose, building routine, and filling time. But our devotion to work can also leave a wake of anguish, with many of its adherents feeling overextended, exhausted, and empty.

The credo that work should be the centerpiece of one's identity quietly governs many stages of modern life. For many children and their parents, it has created a cult of achievement in US education that is feeding an anxiety crisis that is creating a generation of highly anxious kids. For adults, it leads to overwork in the labor force and less time to focus on family, friends, or personal pursuits. For seniors, it has led to an epidemic of loneliness for retirees who are cut off from the jobs that once provided their sole source of community. At the government level, it leads to policies that force Americans to work more than other countries with fewer benefits.

Today, work and workism are facing a double-barreled revolution. There is a revolution in what we do and a revolution in how we do it.

The first revolution is artificial intelligence and automation. I see several reasons to think that the AI revolution is in a headlong sprint. Every few months, we hear about breakthroughs—in solving games, predicting protein shapes, mimicking human language, and synthesizing information. People once believed that machines could replace brawn while creativity was firmly "for humans only." But we may discover that the opposite is true. Text-to-image technology, like DALL-E from the group OpenAI, creates sumptuous and mind-boggling images from simple descriptions. You can type "a raccoon, on a boat, sailing thru the Milky Way, in the style of van

A

Gogh" and within seconds, a machine will generate multiple images that satisfy these requirements. The implications for this kind of program for art, architecture, photography, and video game design are thrilling (and a little terrifying). It may be hard to anticipate what kind of work will be immediately amplified by this technology and what kind of labor will be ultimately replaced by it.

The second revolution is remote and hybrid work. By snipping the tether between work and home, remote work is changing the way that millions of people work, the kind of companies that they start, where they live, and how we collaborate. We are in the very early innings of a work-from-anywhere experiment that was accelerated by the pandemic. It is easy to imagine utopian scenarios. Perhaps the flattening of the job market will make labor equality more equal around the country and around the world. Perhaps the legacies of workplace sexism, ageism, ableism, and racism will come crumbling down with the demise of the office. But it is just as easy to imagine scenarios where the disappearance of the workplace will increase modern anomie and loneliness. If community is "where you keep showing up," then for many people the office is the last community standing. What happens when it goes the way of bowling leagues and weekly church attendance?

In either scenario, I think workism will grow. Mass automation and AI are most likely to replace routine-based work. Many of the jobs left over will include therapists, marketers, influencers, and consultants. These are not the manufacturing jobs of the last century. They are *neuro*-facturing jobs: intellectually intensive labor that is often connected to the Internet and where work can be accomplished on the couch or in the cubicle. With manufacturing jobs, the tools of the office stay at the office. With neurofacturing jobs, the tools are in our minds and thus never physically detach from our bodies. When our minds and computers make it equally easy to work and play online, the workday becomes "leaky," with work trickling into leisure and leisure blending into work. People seem more likely to obsess about their knowledge work after the workday is over and more likely to sew their careers into their identities. As the locus of work has moved from *things we do with our bodies* to *ideas we manipulate with our minds*, our jobs have become the sort of thing that we can think about, literally, all of the time. And many of us do.

I don't like to say that I write about the *future* of work. There is very little discipline in writing about things that haven't happened yet. I prefer to say that I write about the edge of the present. I try to see the world as it is. And then I try to lay out the dominos as they appear to me and suggest scenarios for how the next piece might fall.

This sort of scenario-based writing requires that I think not about the future as a singular point in time, but rather as multiple futures that might proceed from

A

the same set of facts. That may give this book a bit of a choose-your-own-adventure feel. In the following pages, I suggest that AI could replace our jobs, but also that too many Americans are obsessed with our work. I see dangers from too few jobs available and from too much obsession with careers. I see ways for the hybrid office to fail spectacularly and to succeed thrillingly. Do I contradict myself? Very well. The edge of the present is contingent and contradictory.

The book ends with several essays about time. This might seem like a left turn for readers, but it is the natural end point of any discussion about work, life, or attention. Work *is* time. The typical person is alive and conscious for a little under 3,000 weeks. Working 40 hours per week, for 50 weeks per year, for 40 years, the average person spends about 500 entire weeks' worth of time at work. Maybe that feels like a lot to you. But to me, it feels small in context. Work is not everything. It's not even half of life. It's just 500 weeks.

In 2012, the University of Maryland sociologist John P. Robinson reviewed more than 40 years of happiness and time-use surveys that asked Americans how often they felt they were either "rushed" or had "excess time." Perhaps predictably, he concluded that the happiest people were the "never-never" group—those who said they very rarely felt hurried or bored. Their schedules met their energy, and the work they did consumed their attention without exhausting it. On an individual level, happiness means being balanced between busyness and leisure. I think this is true in the biggest picture. I don't hope for a world without work or for a world in which an individual's career becomes the pillar of modern identity. I hope for work without workism.

DEREK THOMPSON

August 2022

A

A WORLD WITHOUT WORK

July 2015

1. Youngstown, USA

The end of work is still just a futuristic concept for most of the United States, but it is something like a moment in history for Youngstown, Ohio, one its residents can cite with precision: September 19, 1977.

For much of the 20th century, Youngstown's steel mills delivered such great prosperity that the city was a model of the American dream, boasting a median income and a homeownership rate that were among the nation's highest. But as manufacturing shifted abroad after World War II, Youngstown steel suffered, and on that gray September afternoon in 1977, Youngstown Sheet and Tube announced the shuttering of its Campbell Works mill. Within five years, the city lost 50,000 jobs and $1.3 billion in manufacturing wages. The effect was so severe that a term was coined to describe the fallout: regional depression.

Youngstown was transformed not only by an economic disruption but also by a psychological and cultural breakdown. Depression, spousal abuse, and suicide all became much more prevalent; the caseload of the area's mental-health center tripled within a decade. The city built four prisons in the mid-1990s—a rare growth industry. One of the few downtown construction projects of that period was a museum dedicated to the defunct steel industry.

In the winter of 2015, I traveled to Ohio to consider what would happen if technology permanently replaced a great deal of human work. I wasn't seeking a tour of our automated future. I went because Youngstown has become a national metaphor for the decline of labor, a place where the middle class of the 20th century has become a museum exhibit.

"Youngstown's story is America's story, because it shows that when jobs go away, the cultural cohesion of a place is destroyed," says John Russo, a professor of labor studies at Youngstown State University. "The cultural breakdown matters even more than the economic breakdown."

Throughout the 21st century, some economists and technologists have worried that it is only a matter of time before computers, automation, and artificial intelligence permanently displace a large share of human work. They see automation high and low—robots in the operating room and at the checkout counter. They imagine self-driving cars snaking through the streets and Amazon drones dotting the sky, replacing millions of drivers, warehouse stockers, and retail workers. They see new AI tools mimicking human speech, art, and thought. They observe that the capabilities of machines—already formidable—continue to expand exponentially, while our own remain the same. And they wonder: Is any job truly safe?

Futurists and science-fiction writers have at times looked forward to machines' workplace takeover with a kind of giddy excitement, imagining the banishment of drudgery and its replacement by expansive leisure and almost limitless personal freedom. And make no mistake: if the capabilities of computers continue to multiply while the price of computing continues to decline, that will mean a great many of life's necessities and luxuries will become ever cheaper, and it will mean great wealth—at least when aggregated up to the level of the national economy.

But even leaving aside questions of how to distribute that wealth, the widespread disappearance of work would usher in a social transformation unlike any we've seen. If John Russo is right, then saving work is more important than saving any particular job. Industriousness has served as America's unofficial religion since its founding. The sanctity and preeminence of work lie at the heart of the country's politics, economics, and social interactions. What might happen if work goes away?

THE US LABOR FORCE has been shaped by millennia of technological progress. Agricultural technology birthed the farming industry, the Industrial Revolution moved people into factories, and then globalization and automation moved them back out, giving rise to a nation of services. But throughout these reshufflings, the total number of jobs has always increased. What may be looming is something different: an era of technological unemployment, in which computer scientists and software engineers essentially invent us out of work, and the total number of jobs declines steadily and permanently.

This fear is not new. The hope that machines might free us from toil has always been intertwined with the fear that they will rob us of our agency. During the Great Depression, President Herbert Hoover received a letter warning that industrial technology was a "Frankenstein monster" that threatened to upend manufacturing, "devouring our civilization." (The letter came from the mayor of Palo Alto, of all places.) In 1962, President John F. Kennedy said, "If men have the talent to invent new machines that put men out of work, they have the talent to put those men back to work." But two years later, a committee of scientists and social activists sent an open letter to President Lyndon B. Johnson arguing that "the cybernation revolution" would create "a separate nation of the poor, the unskilled, the jobless," who would be unable either to find work or to afford life's necessities.

The end-of-work argument has often been dismissed as the "Luddite fallacy," an allusion to the 19th-century British brutes who smashed textile-making machines at the dawn of the Industrial Revolution, fearing the machines would put hand-weavers out of work. But some of the most sober economists are beginning to worry that the Luddites weren't wrong, just premature. When former Treasury Secretary Lawrence Summers was an MIT undergraduate in the early 1970s, many economists disdained "the stupid people [who] thought that automation was going to make all the jobs go away," he said at the National Bureau of Economic Research Summer Institute in July 2013. "Until a few years ago, I didn't think this was a very complicated subject: The Luddites were wrong, and the believers in technology and technological progress were right. I'm not so completely certain now."

2. Reasons to Cry Robot

What does the "end of work" mean, exactly? It does not mean the imminence of total unemployment, nor is the United States remotely likely to face, say, 30 or 50 percent unemployment within the next decade. Rather, technology could exert a slow but continual downward pressure on the value and availability of work—that is, on wages and on the share of prime-age workers with full-time jobs. Eventually, by degrees, that could create a new normal, where the expectation that work will be a central feature of adult life dissipates for a significant portion of society.

One common objection to the idea that technology will permanently displace huge numbers of workers is that new gadgets, like self-checkout kiosks at drugstores, have failed to fully displace their human counterparts, like cashiers. But employers typically take years to embrace new machines at the expense of workers. The robotics revolution began in factories in the 1960s and '70s, but manufacturing employment kept rising until 1980, and then collapsed during the subsequent recessions. Likewise, "the personal computer existed in the '80s," says Henry Siu, an economist at the University of British Columbia, "but you don't see any effect on office and administrative-support jobs until the 1990s, and then suddenly, in the last recession, it's huge. So today you've got checkout screens and the promise of driverless cars, flying drones, and little warehouse robots. We know that these tasks can be done by machines rather than people. But we may not see the effect until the next recession, or the recession after that."

Some observers say our humanity is a moat that machines cannot cross. They believe people's capacity for compassion, deep understanding, and creativity is inimitable. But as Erik Brynjolfsson and Andrew McAfee have argued in their book *The Second Machine Age*, computers are so dexterous that predicting their application 10 years from now is almost impossible. Who could have guessed in 2005, two years before the iPhone was released, that smartphones would threaten hotel jobs within the decade,

A

by helping homeowners rent out their apartments and houses to strangers on Airbnb? Or that AI researchers would develop a technology, like DALL-E, that could provide complex high-quality illustrations by demand?

In 2013, Oxford University researchers forecast that machines might be able to perform half of all US jobs in the next two decades. The projection was audacious, but in at least a few cases, it probably didn't go far enough. For example, the authors named psychologist as one of the occupations least likely to be "computerisable." But some research suggests that people are more honest in therapy sessions when they believe they are confessing their troubles to a computer, because a machine can't pass moral judgment. Google and WebMD already may be answering questions once reserved for one's therapist. This doesn't prove that psychologists are going the way of the textile worker. Rather, it shows how easily computers can encroach on areas previously considered "for humans only."

AFTER 300 YEARS OF breathtaking innovation, people aren't massively unemployed or indentured by machines. But to suggest how this could change, some economists have pointed to the defunct career of the second-most-important species in US economic history: the horse.

For many centuries, people created technologies that made the horse more productive and more valuable—like plows for agriculture and swords for battle. One might have assumed that the continuing advance of complementary technologies would make the animal ever more essential to farming and fighting, historically perhaps the two most consequential human activities. Instead came inventions that made the horse obsolete—the tractor, the car, and the tank. After tractors rolled onto American farms in the early 20th century, the population of horses and mules began to decline steeply, falling nearly 50 percent by the 1930s and 90 percent by the 1950s.

Humans can do much more than trot, carry, and pull. But the skills required in most offices hardly elicit our full range of intelligence. Most jobs are still boring, repetitive, and easily learned. The most common occupations in the United States are retail salesperson, cashier, food and beverage server, and office clerk. Together, these four jobs employ 15.4 million people—nearly 10 percent of the labor force, or more workers than there are in Texas and Massachusetts combined. Each is highly susceptible to automation, according to the Oxford study.

Technology creates some jobs too, but the creative half of creative destruction is easily overstated. Nine out of 10 workers today are in occupations that existed 100 years ago, and just 5 percent of the jobs generated between 1993 and 2013 came from "high tech" sectors like computing, software, and telecommunications. Our newest industries tend to be the most labor-efficient: they don't require

A

nearly as many people to produce the same value. In 1964, the nation's most valuable company, AT&T, was worth $267 billion in today's dollars and employed 758,611 people. Today's telecommunications giant, Google, is worth $1.5 trillion and has 150,000 employees—five times the value with one-fifth of the workforce. It is for precisely this reason that the economic historian Robert Skidelsky, comparing the exponential growth in computing power with the less-than-exponential growth in job complexity, has said, "Sooner or later, we will run out of jobs."

Is that certain—or certainly imminent? No. The signs so far are murky and suggestive. The most fundamental and wrenching job restructurings and contractions tend to happen during recessions: We'll know more after the next couple of downturns. But the possibility seems significant enough—and the consequences disruptive enough—that we owe it to ourselves to start thinking about what society could look like without universal work, in an effort to begin nudging it toward the better outcomes and away from the worse ones.

To paraphrase the science-fiction novelist William Gibson, there are, perhaps, fragments of the post-work future distributed throughout the present. I see three overlapping possibilities as formal employment opportunities decline. Some people displaced from the formal workforce will devote their freedom to simple leisure; some will seek to build productive communities outside the workplace; and others will fight, passionately and in many cases fruitlessly, to reclaim their productivity by piecing together jobs in an informal economy. These are futures of consumption, communal creativity, and contingency. In any combination, it is almost certain that the country would have to embrace a radical new role for government.

3. Consumption: The Paradox of Leisure

Work is really three things, says Peter Frase, the author of *Four Futures,* a book about how automation will change America: the means by which the economy produces goods, the means by which people earn income, and an activity that lends meaning or purpose to many people's lives. "We tend to conflate these things," he told me, "because today we need to pay people to keep the lights on, so to speak. But in a future of abundance, you wouldn't, and we ought to think about ways to make it easier and better to not be employed."

Frase belongs to a small group of writers, academics, and economists—they have been called "post-workists"—who welcome, even root for, the end of labor. American society has "an irrational belief in work for work's sake," says Benjamin Hunnicutt, another post-workist and a historian at the University of Iowa, even though most jobs aren't so uplifting. A 2014 Gallup report of worker satisfaction found that as many as 70 percent of Americans don't feel engaged by their current job. Hunnicutt told me that if a cashier's work were a video game—grab an item, find the bar code, scan it, slide the item onward, and repeat—critics of video games might call it mindless. But when it's a job, politicians praise its intrinsic dignity. "Purpose, meaning, identity, fulfillment, creativity, autonomy—all these things that positive psychology has shown us to be necessary for well-being are absent in the average job," he said.

The post-workists are certainly right about some important things. Paid labor does not always map to social good. Raising children and caring for the sick is essential work, and these jobs are compensated poorly or not at all. In a post-work society, Hunnicutt said, people might spend more time caring for their families and neighbors; pride could come from our relationships rather than from our careers.

The post-work proponents acknowledge that, even in the best post-work scenarios, pride and jealousy will persevere, because reputation will always be scarce, even in an economy of abundance. But with the right government provisions, they believe, the end of wage labor will allow for a golden age of well-being. Hunnicutt said he thinks colleges could reemerge as cultural centers rather than job-prep institutions. The word *school*, he pointed out, comes from *skholē*, the Greek word for "leisure." "We used to teach people to be free," he said. "Now we teach them to work."

Hunnicutt's vision rests on certain assumptions about taxation and redistribution that might not be congenial to many Americans today. But even leaving that aside for the moment, this vision is problematic: It doesn't resemble the world as it is currently experienced by most jobless people. By and large, the jobless don't spend their downtime socializing with friends or taking up new hobbies. Instead, they watch TV or sleep. Time-use surveys show that jobless prime-age people dedicate some of the time once spent working to cleaning and childcare. But men in particular devote most of their free time to leisure, the lion's share of which is spent watching television, browsing the Internet, and sleeping. Retired seniors watch about 50 hours of television a week, according to Nielsen. That means they spend a majority of their lives either sleeping or sitting on the sofa looking at a flatscreen. The unemployed theoretically have the most time to socialize, and yet studies have shown that they feel the most social isolation; it is surprisingly hard to replace the camaraderie of the water cooler.

Most people want to work, and are miserable when they cannot. The ills of unemployment go well beyond the loss of income; people who lose their job are more likely to suffer from mental and physical ailments. "There is a loss of status, a general malaise and demoralization, which

A

appears somatically or psychologically or both," says Ralph Catalano, a public health professor at UC Berkeley. Research has shown that it is harder to recover from a long bout of joblessness than from losing a loved one or suffering a life-altering injury. The very things that help many people recover from other emotional traumas—a routine, an absorbing distraction, a daily purpose—are not readily available to the unemployed.

The transition from labor force to leisure force would likely be particularly hard on Americans, the worker bees of the rich world: Between 1950 and 2012, annual hours worked per worker fell significantly throughout Europe—by about 40 percent in Germany and the Netherlands—but by only 10 percent in the United States. Richer, college-educated Americans are working more than they did 30 years ago, particularly when you count time working and answering email at home.

In 1989, the psychologists Mihaly Csikszentmihalyi and Judith LeFevre conducted a famous study of Chicago workers that found people at work often wished they were somewhere else. But in questionnaires, these same workers reported feeling better and less anxious in the office or at the plant than they did elsewhere. The two psychologists called this "the paradox of work": many people are happier complaining about jobs than they are luxuriating in too much leisure. Other researchers have used the term "guilty couch potato" to describe people who use media to relax but often feel worthless when they reflect on their unproductive downtime. Contentment speaks in the present tense, but something more—pride—comes only in reflection on past accomplishments.

The post-workists argue that Americans work so hard because their culture has conditioned them to feel guilty when they are not being productive, and that this guilt will fade as work ceases to be the norm. This might prove true, but it's an untestable hypothesis. When I asked Hunnicutt what sort of modern community most resembles his ideal of a post-work society, he admitted, "I'm not sure that such a place exists."

Less passive and more nourishing forms of mass leisure could develop. Arguably, they already are developing. The Internet, social media, and gaming offer entertainments that are as easy to slip into as is watching TV, but all are more purposeful and often less isolating. Video games, despite the derision aimed at them, are vehicles for achievement of a sort. Jeremy Bailenson, a communications professor at Stanford, says that as virtual reality technology improves, people's "cyber-existence" will become as rich and social as their "real" life. Games in which users climb "into another person's skin to embody his or her experiences firsthand" don't just let people live out vicarious fantasies, he has argued, but also "help you live as somebody else to teach you empathy and pro-social skills."

But it's hard to imagine that leisure could ever entirely fill the vacuum of accomplishment left by the demise of labor. Most people do need to achieve things through, yes, work, to feel a lasting sense of purpose. To envision a future that offers more than minute-to-minute satisfaction, we have to imagine how millions of people might find meaningful work without formal wages. So, inspired by the predictions of one of America's most famous labor economists, I took a detour on my way to Youngstown and stopped in Columbus, Ohio.

4. Communal Creativity: The Artisans' Revenge

Artisans made up the original American middle class. Before industrialization swept through the US economy, many people who didn't work on farms were silversmiths, blacksmiths, or woodworkers. These artisans were ground up by the machinery of mass production in the 20th century. But Lawrence Katz, a labor economist at Harvard, sees the next wave of automation returning us to an age of craftsmanship and artistry. In particular, he looks forward to the ramifications of 3D printing, whereby machines construct complex objects from digital designs.

The factories that arose more than a century ago "could make Model Ts and forks and knives and mugs and glasses in a standardized, cheap way, and that drove the artisans out of business," Katz told me. "But what if the new tech, like 3-D-printing machines, can do customized things that are almost as cheap? It's possible that information technology and robots eliminate traditional jobs and make possible a new artisanal economy . . . an economy geared around self-expression, where people would do artistic things with their time."

In other words, it would be a future not of consumption but of creativity, as technology returns the tools of the assembly line to individuals, democratizing the means of mass production.

Something like this future is already present in the small but growing number of industrial shops called "makerspaces" that have popped up in the United States and around the world. The Columbus Idea Foundry is the country's largest such space, a cavernous, converted shoe factory stocked with industrial-age machinery. Several hundred members pay a monthly fee to use its arsenal of machines to make gifts and jewelry; weld, finish, and paint; play with plasma cutters and work an angle grinder; or operate a lathe with a machinist.

When I arrived there on a bitterly cold afternoon in February of 2015, a chalkboard standing on an easel by the door displayed three arrows, pointing toward BATHROOMS, PEWTER CASTING, and ZOMBIES. Near the entrance, three men with black fingertips and grease-stained shirts took

A

turns fixing a 60-year-old metal-turning lathe. Behind them, a resident artist was tutoring an older woman on how to transfer her photographs onto a large canvas, while a couple of guys fed pizza pies into a propane-fired stone oven. Elsewhere, men in protective goggles welded a sign for a local chicken restaurant, while others punched codes into a computer-controlled laser-cutting machine. Beneath the din of drilling and woodcutting, a Pandora rock station hummed tinnily from a Wi-Fi-connected Edison phonograph horn. The foundry is not just a gymnasium of tools. It is a social center.

Alex Bandar, who started the foundry after receiving a doctorate in materials science and engineering, has a theory about the rhythms of invention in American history. Over the past century, he told me, the economy has moved from hardware to software, from atoms to bits, and people have spent more time at work in front of screens. But as computers take over more tasks previously considered the province of humans, the pendulum will swing back from bits to atoms, at least when it comes to how people spend their days. Bandar thinks that a digitally preoccupied society will come to appreciate the pure and distinct pleasure of making things you can touch. "I've always wanted to usher in a new era of technology where robots do our bidding," Bandar said. "If you have better batteries, better robotics, more dexterous manipulation, then it's not a far stretch to say robots do most of the work. So what do we do? Play? Draw? Actually talk to each other again?"

You don't need any particular fondness for plasma cutters to see the beauty of an economy where tens of millions of people make things they enjoy making—whether physical or digital, in buildings or in online communities—and receive feedback and appreciation for their work. The Internet and the cheap availability of artistic tools have already empowered millions of people to produce culture from their living rooms. People upload more than 400,000 hours of YouTube videos and 350 million new Facebook photos every day. The demise of the formal economy could free many would-be artists, writers, and craftspeople to dedicate their time to creative interests—to live as cultural producers. Such activities offer virtues that many organizational psychologists consider central to satisfaction at work: independence, the chance to develop mastery, and a sense of purpose.

After touring the foundry, I sat at a long table with several members, sharing the pizza that had come out of the communal oven. I asked them what they thought of their organization as a model for a future where automation reached further into the formal economy. A mixed-media artist named Kate Morgan said that most people she knew at the foundry would quit their jobs and use the foundry to start their own business if they could. Others

A

spoke about the fundamental need to witness the outcome of one's work, which was satisfied more deeply by craftsmanship than by other jobs they'd held.

Late in the conversation, we were joined by Terry Griner, an engineer who had built miniature steam engines in his garage before Bandar invited him to join the foundry. His fingers were covered in soot, and he told me about the pride he had in his ability to fix things. "I've been working since I was 16. I've done food service, restaurant work, hospital work, and computer programming. I've done a lot of different jobs," said Griner, who is now a divorced father. "But if we had a society that said, 'We'll cover your essentials, you can work in the shop,' I think that would be utopia. That, to me, would be the best of all possible worlds."

5. Contingency: "You're on Your Own"

One mile to the east of downtown Youngstown, in a brick building surrounded by several empty lots, is Royal Oaks, an iconic blue-collar dive. At about 5:30 p.m. on a Wednesday, the place was nearly full. The bar glowed yellow and green from the lights mounted along a wall. Old beer signs, trophies, masks, and mannequins cluttered the back corner of the main room, like party leftovers stuffed in an attic. The scene was mostly middle-aged men, some in groups, talking loudly about baseball and smelling vaguely of pot; some drank alone at the bar, sitting quietly or listening to music on headphones. I spoke with several patrons there who work as musicians, artists, or handymen; many did not hold a steady job.

"It is the end of a particular kind of wage work," said Hannah Woodroofe, a bartender there who, it turns out, is also a graduate student at the University of Chicago. (She's writing a dissertation on Youngstown as a harbinger of the future of work.) A lot of people in the city make ends meet via "post-wage arrangements," she said, working for tenancy or under the table, or trading services. Places like Royal Oaks are the new union halls: People go there not only to relax but also to find tradespeople for particular jobs, like auto repair. Others go to exchange fresh vegetables, grown in urban gardens they've created amid Youngstown's vacant lots.

When an entire area, like Youngstown, suffers from high and prolonged unemployment, problems caused by unemployment move beyond the personal sphere; widespread joblessness shatters neighborhoods and leaches away their civic spirit. John Russo, the Youngstown State professor, who is a co-author of a history of the city, *Steeltown U.S.A.*, says the local identity took a savage blow when residents lost the ability to find reliable employment. "I can't stress this enough: this isn't just about economics; it's psychological," he told me.

Russo sees Youngstown as the leading edge of a larger trend toward the development of what he calls the "precariat"—a working class that swings from task to task in order to make ends meet and suffers a loss of labor rights, bargaining rights, and job security. In Youngstown, many of these workers have by now made their peace with insecurity and poverty by building an identity, and some measure of pride, around contingency. The faith they lost in institutions—the corporations that have abandoned the city, the police who have failed to keep them safe—has not returned. But Russo and Woodroofe both told me they put stock in their own independence. And so a place that once defined itself single-mindedly by the steel its residents made has gradually learned to embrace the valorization of well-rounded resourcefulness.

Karen Schubert, a 54-year-old writer with two master's degrees, accepted a part-time job as a hostess at a café in Youngstown early this year, after spending months searching for full-time work. Schubert, who has two grown children and an infant grandson, said she'd loved teaching writing and literature at the local university. But many colleges have replaced full-time professors with part-time adjuncts in order to control costs, and she'd found that with the hours she could get, adjunct teaching didn't pay a living wage, so she'd stopped. "I think I would feel like a personal failure if I didn't know that so many Americans have their leg caught in the same trap," she said.

Among Youngstown's precariat, one can see a third possible future, where millions of people struggle for years to build a sense of purpose in the absence of formal jobs, and where entrepreneurship emerges out of necessity. But while it lacks the comforts of the consumption economy or the cultural richness of Lawrence Katz's artisanal future, it is more complex than an outright dystopia. "There are young people working part-time in the new economy who feel independent, whose work and personal relationships are contingent, and say they like it like this—to have short hours so they have time to focus on their passions," Russo said.

Schubert's wages at the café are not enough to live on, and in her spare time, she sells books of her poetry at readings and organizes gatherings of the literary-arts community in Youngstown, where other writers (many of them also underemployed) share their prose. The evaporation of work has deepened the local arts and music scene, several residents told me, because people who are inclined toward the arts have so much time to spend with one another. "We're a devastatingly poor and hemorrhaging population, but the people who live here are fearless and creative and phenomenal," Schubert said.

Whether or not one has artistic ambitions as Schubert does, it is arguably growing easier to find short-term gigs or spot employment. Paradoxically, technology is the reason. A constellation of Internet-enabled companies matches available workers with quick jobs, most prominently including Uber (for drivers), Seamless (for meal deliverers), Homejoy (for house cleaners), and TaskRabbit (for just about anyone else). And online markets like Craigslist and eBay have likewise made it easier for people to take on small independent projects, such as furniture refurbishing. Although the on-demand economy is not yet a major part of the employment picture, the number of "temporary-help services" workers has grown by 50 percent since 2010, according to the Bureau of Labor Statistics.

Some of these services, too, could be usurped, eventually, by machines. But on-demand apps also spread the work around by carving up jobs, like driving a taxi, into hundreds of little tasks, like a single drive, which allows more people to compete for smaller pieces of work. These new arrangements are already challenging the legal definitions of employer and employee, and there are many reasons to be ambivalent about them. But if the future involves a declining number of full-time jobs, as in Youngstown, then splitting some of the remaining work up among many part-time workers, instead of a few full-timers, wouldn't necessarily be a bad development. We shouldn't be too quick to excoriate companies that let people combine their work, art, and leisure in whatever ways they choose.

Today the norm is to think about employment and unemployment as a black-and-white binary, rather than two points at opposite ends of a wide spectrum of working arrangements. As late as the mid-19th century, though, the modern concept of "unemployment" didn't exist in the United States. Most people lived on farms, and while paid work came and went, home industry—canning, sewing, carpentry—was a constant. Even in the worst economic panics, people typically found productive things to do. The despondency and helplessness of unemployment were discovered, to the bafflement and dismay of cultural critics, only after factory work became dominant and cities swelled.

The 21st century, if it presents fewer full-time jobs in the sectors that can be automated, could in this respect come to resemble the mid-19th century: an economy marked by episodic work across a range of activities, the loss of any one of which would not make somebody suddenly idle. Many bristle that contingent gigs offer a devil's bargain—a bit of additional autonomy in exchange for a larger loss of security. But some might thrive in a market where versatility and hustle are rewarded—where there are, as in Youngstown, few jobs to have, yet many things to do.

A

6. Government: The Visible Hand

In the 1950s, Henry Ford II, the CEO of Ford, and Walter Reuther, the head of the United Auto Workers union, were touring a new engine plant in Cleveland. Ford gestured to a fleet of machines and said, "Walter, how are you going to get these robots to pay union dues?" The union boss famously replied: "Henry, how are you going to get them to buy your cars?"

As Martin Ford (no relation) writes in his new book, *The Rise of the Robots*, this story might be apocryphal, but its message is instructive. We're pretty good at noticing the immediate effects of technology's substituting for workers, such as fewer people on the factory floor. What's harder is anticipating the second-order effects of this transformation, such as what happens to the consumer economy when you take away the consumers.

The decline of the labor force would make our politics more contentious. Deciding how to tax profits and distribute income could become the most significant economic-policy debate in American history. In *The Wealth of Nations*, Adam Smith used the term invisible hand to refer to the order and social benefits that arise, surprisingly, from individuals' selfish actions. But to preserve the consumer economy and the social fabric, governments might have to embrace what Haruhiko Kuroda, the governor of the Bank of Japan, has called the visible hand of economic intervention. What follows is an early sketch of how it all might work.

In the near term, local governments might do well to create more and more ambitious community centers or other public spaces where residents can meet, learn skills, bond around sports or crafts, and socialize. Two of the most common side effects of unemployment are loneliness, on the individual level, and the hollowing-out of community pride. A national policy that directed money toward centers in distressed areas might remedy the maladies of idleness, and form the beginnings of a long-term experiment on how to reengage people in their neighborhoods in the absence of full employment.

We could also make it easier for people to start their own, small-scale (and even part-time) businesses. New-business formation has declined in the past few decades in all 50 states. One way to nurture fledgling ideas would be to build out a network of business incubators. Here Youngstown offers an unexpected model: its business incubator has been recognized internationally, and its success has brought new hope to West Federal Street, the city's main drag.

Near the beginning of any broad decline in job availability, the United States might take a lesson from Germany on job-sharing. The German government gives firms incentives to cut all their workers' hours rather than lay off some of them during hard times. So a company

A

with 50 workers that might otherwise lay off 10 people instead reduces everyone's hours by 20 percent. Such a policy would help workers at established firms keep their attachment to the labor force despite the declining amount of overall labor.

Spreading work in this way has its limits. Some jobs can't be easily shared, and in any case, sharing jobs wouldn't stop labor's pie from shrinking: It would only apportion the slices differently. Eventually, Washington would have to somehow spread wealth, too.

One way of doing that would be to more heavily tax the growing share of income going to the owners of capital, and use the money to cut checks to all adults. This idea—called a "universal basic income"—has received bipartisan support in the past. Many liberals currently support it, and in the 1960s, Richard Nixon and the conservative economist Milton Friedman each proposed a version of the idea. That history notwithstanding, the politics of universal income in a world without universal work would be daunting. The rich could say, with some accuracy, that their hard work was subsidizing the idleness of millions of "takers." What's more, although a universal income might replace lost wages, it would do little to preserve the social benefits of work.

The most direct solution to the latter problem would be for the government to pay people to do something, rather than nothing. Although this smacks of old European socialism, or Depression-era "makework," it might do the most to preserve virtues such as responsibility, agency, and industriousness. In the 1930s, the Works Progress Administration did more than rebuild the nation's infrastructure. It hired 40,000 artists and other cultural workers to produce music and theater, murals and paintings, state and regional travel guides, and surveys of state records. It's not impossible to imagine something like the WPA—or an effort even more capacious—for a post-work future.

What might that look like? Several national projects might justify direct hiring, such as caring for a rising population of elderly people. But if the balance of work continues to shift toward the small-bore and episodic, the simplest way to help everybody stay busy might be government sponsorship of a national online marketplace of work (or, alternatively, a series of local ones, sponsored by local governments). Individuals could browse for large long-term projects, like cleaning up after a natural disaster, or small short-term ones: an hour of tutoring, an evening of entertainment, an art commission. The requests could come from local governments or community associations or nonprofit groups; from rich families seeking nannies or tutors; or from other individuals given some number of credits to "spend" on the site each year. To ensure a baseline level of attachment to the workforce, the government could pay adults a flat rate in return for some

A

minimum level of activity on the site, but people could always earn more by taking on more gigs.

Although a digital WPA might strike some people as a strange anachronism, it would be similar to a federalized version of Mechanical Turk, the popular Amazon sister site where individuals and companies post projects of varying complexity, while so-called Turks on the other end browse tasks and collect money for the ones they complete. Mechanical Turk was designed to list tasks that cannot be performed by a computer. (The name is an allusion to an 18th-century Austrian hoax, in which a famous automaton that seemed to play masterful chess concealed a human player who chose the moves and moved the pieces.)

A government marketplace might likewise specialize in those tasks that required empathy, humanity, or a personal touch. By connecting millions of people in one central hub, it might even inspire what the technology writer Robin Sloan has called "a Cambrian explosion of megascale creative and intellectual pursuits, a generation of Wikipedia-scale projects that can ask their users for even deeper commitments."

THERE'S A CASE TO be made for using the tools of government to provide other incentives as well, to help people avoid the typical traps of joblessness and build rich lives and vibrant communities. After all, the members of the

Columbus Idea Foundry probably weren't born with an innate love of lathe operation or laser-cutting. Mastering these skills requires discipline; discipline requires an education; and an education, for many people, involves the expectation that hours of often frustrating practice will eventually prove rewarding. In a post-work society, the financial rewards of education and training won't be as obvious. This is a singular challenge of imagining a flourishing post-work society: How will people discover their talents, or the rewards that come from expertise, if they don't see much incentive to develop either?

Modest payments to young people for attending and completing college, skills-training programs, or community-center workshops might eventually be worth considering. This seems radical, but the aim would be conservative—to preserve the status quo of an educated and engaged society. Whatever their career opportunities, young people will still grow up to be citizens, neighbors, and even, episodically, workers. Nudges toward education and training might be particularly beneficial to men, who are more likely to withdraw into their living rooms when they become unemployed.

7. Jobs and Callings

Decades from now, perhaps the 20th century will strike future historians as an aberration, with its religious devotion to overwork in a time of prosperity, its attenuations of family in service to job opportunity, its conflation of income with self-worth. The post-work society I've described holds a warped mirror up to today's economy, but in many ways it reflects the forgotten norms of the mid-19th century—the artisan middle class, the primacy of local communities, and the unfamiliarity with widespread joblessness.

The three potential futures of consumption, communal creativity, and contingency are not separate paths branching out from the present. They're likely to intertwine and even influence one another. Entertainment will surely become more immersive and exert a gravitational pull on people without much to do. But if that's all that happens, society will have failed. The foundry in Columbus shows how the "third places" in people's lives (communities separate from their homes and offices) could become central to growing up, learning new skills, discovering passions. And with or without such places, many people will need to embrace the resourcefulness learned over time by cities like Youngstown, which, even if they seem like museum exhibits of an old economy, might foretell the future for many more cities in the next 25 years.

On my last day in Youngstown, I met with Howard Jesko, a 60-year-old Youngstown State graduate student, at a burger joint along the main street. A few months after Black Friday in 1977, as a senior at Ohio State University,

Jesko received a phone call from his father, a specialty-hose manufacturer near Youngstown. "Don't bother coming back here for a job," his dad said. "There aren't going to be any left." Years later, Jesko returned to Youngstown to work, but he recently quit his job selling products like waterproofing systems to construction companies; his customers had been devastated by the Great Recession and weren't buying much anymore. Around the same time, a left knee replacement due to degenerative arthritis resulted in a 10-day hospital stay, which gave him time to think about the future. Jesko decided to go back to school to become a professor. "My true calling," he told me, "has always been to teach."

One theory of work holds that people tend to see themselves in jobs, careers, or callings. Individuals who say their work is "just a job" emphasize that they are working for money rather than aligning themselves with any higher purpose. Those with pure careerist ambitions are focused not only on income but also on the status that comes with promotions and the growing renown of their peers. But one pursues a calling not only for pay or status, but also for the intrinsic fulfillment of the work itself.

When I think about the role that work plays in people's self-esteem—particularly in America—the prospect of a no-work future seems hopeless. There is no universal basic income that can prevent the civic ruin of a country built on a handful of workers permanently subsidizing the idleness of tens of millions of people. But a future of less work still holds a glint of hope, because the necessity of salaried jobs now prevents so many from seeking immersive activities that they enjoy.

After my conversation with Jesko, I walked back to my car to drive out of Youngstown. I thought about Jesko's life as it might have been had Youngstown's steel mills never given way to a steel museum—had the city continued to provide stable, predictable careers to its residents. If Jesko had taken a job in the steel industry, he might be preparing for retirement today. Instead, that industry collapsed and then, years later, another recession struck. The outcome of this cumulative grief is that Howard Jesko is not retiring at 60. He's getting his master's degree to become a teacher. It took the loss of so many jobs to force him to pursue the work he always wanted to do.

THE RELIGION OF WORKISM

February 2019

IN HIS 1930 ESSAY "Economic Possibilities for Our Grand-children," the economist John Maynard Keynes predicted a 15-hour workweek in the 21st century, creating the equivalent of a five-day weekend. "For the first time since his creation man will be faced with his real, his permanent problem," Keynes wrote, "how to occupy the leisure."

This became a popular view. In a 1957 article in *The New York Times*, the writer Erik Barnouw predicted that, as work became easier, our identity would be defined by our hobbies, or our family life. "The increasingly auto-matic nature of many jobs, coupled with the shortening work week [leads] an increasing number of workers to look not to work but to leisure for satisfaction, meaning, expression," he wrote.

These post-work predictions weren't entirely wrong. By some counts, Americans work much less than they used to. The average work year has shrunk by more than 200 hours since the 1950s. But those figures don't tell the whole story. Rich, college-educated people—especially men—work more than they did many decades ago. They are reared from their teenage years to make their passion their career and, if they don't have a calling, told not to yield until they find one.

The economists of the early 20th century did not foresee that work might evolve from a means of material production to a means of identity production. They failed to anticipate that, for the poor and middle class, work would remain a necessity; but for the college-educated elite, it would morph into a kind of religion, promising identity, transcendence, and community. Call it workism.

1. The Gospel of Work

The decline of traditional faith in America has coincided with an explosion of new atheisms. Some people worship beauty, some worship political identities, and others worship their children. But everybody worships something. And workism is among the most potent of the new religions competing for congregants.

What is workism? It is the belief that work is not only necessary to economic production, but also the centerpiece of one's identity and life's purpose; and the belief that any policy to promote human welfare must always encourage more work.

Homo industrious is not new to the American landscape. The American dream—that hoary mythology that hard work always guarantees upward mobility—has for more than a century made the US obsessed with material success and the exhaustive striving required to earn it.

No large country in the world as productive as the United States averages more hours of work a year. And the gap between the US and other countries is growing. Between 1950 and 2012, annual hours worked per employee fell by about 40 percent in Germany and the Netherlands—but by only 10 percent in the United States. Americans "work longer hours, have shorter vacations, get less in unemployment, disability, and retirement benefits, and retire later, than people in comparably rich societies," wrote Samuel P. Huntington in his 2005 book, *Who Are We? The Challenges to America's National Identity.*

One group has led the widening of the workist gap: rich men.

In 1980, the highest-earning men actually worked fewer hours per week than middle-class and low-income men, according to a survey by the Minneapolis Fed. But that's changed. By 2005, the richest 10 percent of married men had the longest average workweek. In that same time, college-educated men reduced their leisure time more than any other group. Today, it is fair to say that elite American men have transformed themselves into the world's premier workaholics, toiling longer hours than both poorer men in the US and rich men in similarly rich countries.

A

This shift defies economic logic—and economic history. The rich have always worked less than the poor, because they could afford to. The landed gentry of pre-industrial Europe dined, danced, and gossiped, while serfs toiled without end. In the early 20th century, rich Americans used their ample downtime to buy weekly movie tickets and dabble in sports. Today's rich American men can afford vastly more downtime. But they have used their wealth to buy the strangest of prizes: more work!

Perhaps long hours are part of an arms race for status and income among the moneyed elite. Or maybe the logic here isn't economic at all. It's emotional—even spiritual. The best-educated and highest-earning Americans, who can have whatever they want, have chosen the office for the same reason that devout Christians attend church on Sundays: It's where they feel most themselves. "For many of today's rich there is no such thing as 'leisure'; in the classic sense—work is their play," the economist Robert Frank wrote in *The Wall Street Journal*. "Building wealth to them is a creative process, and the closest thing they have to fun."

Workism may have started with rich men, but the ethos is spreading—across gender and age. In a 2018 paper on elite universities, researchers found that for women, the most important benefit of attending a selective college isn't higher wages, but more hours at the office. In other words, our elite institutions are minting coed workists. What's more, in a recent Pew Research report on the epidemic of youth anxiety, 95 percent of teens said "having a job or career they enjoy" would be "extremely or very important" to them as an adult. This ranked higher than any other priority, including "helping other people who are in need" (81 percent) or getting married (47 percent). Finding meaning at work beats family and kindness as the top ambition of today's young people.

Even as Americans worship workism, its leaders consecrate it from the marble daises of Congress and enshrine it in law. Most advanced countries give new parents paid leave; but the United States guarantees no such thing. Many advanced countries ease the burden of parenthood with national policies; but US public spending on child care and early education is near the bottom of international rankings. In most advanced countries, citizens are guaranteed access to health care by their government; but the majority of insured Americans get health care through— where else?—their workplace. Automation and AI may soon threaten the labor force, but America's welfare system has become more work-based in the past 20 years. In 1996, President Bill Clinton signed the Personal Responsibility and Work Opportunity Reconciliation Act, which replaced much of the existing welfare system with programs that made benefits contingent on the recipient's employment.

A

The religion of work isn't just a cultist feature of America's elite. It's also the law.

HERE'S A FAIR QUESTION: Is there anything wrong with hard, even obsessive, work?

Humankind has not invented itself out of labor. Machine intelligence isn't ready to run the world's factories, or care for the sick. In every advanced economy, most prime-age people who can work do—and in poorer countries, the average workweek is even longer than in the United States. Without work, including non-salaried labor like raising a child, most people tend to feel miserable. Some evidence suggests that long-term unemployment is even more wrenching than losing a loved one, since the absence of an engaging distraction removes the very thing that tends to provide solace to mourners in the first place.

There is nothing wrong with work, when work must be done. And there is no question that an elite obsession with meaningful work will produce a handful of winners who hit the workist lottery: busy, rich, and deeply fulfilled. But a culture that funnels its dreams of self-actualization into salaried jobs is setting itself up for collective anxiety, mass disappointment, and inevitable burnout.

In the past century, the American conception of work has shifted from jobs to careers to callings—from necessity to status to meaning. In an agrarian or early manufacturing economy, where tens of millions of people perform similar routinized tasks, there are no delusions about the higher purpose of, say, planting corn or screwing bolts: It's just a job.

The rise of the professional class and corporate bureaucracies in the early 20th century created the modern journey of a career, a narrative arc bending toward a set of precious initials: VP, SVP, CEO. The upshot is that for today's workists, anything short of finding one's vocational soul mate means a wasted life.

"We've created this idea that the meaning of life should be found in work," says Oren Cass, the author of the book *The Once and Future Worker*. "We tell young people that their work should be their passion. 'Don't give up until you find a job that you love!' we say. 'You should be changing the world!' we tell them. That is the message in commencement addresses, in pop culture, and frankly, in media, including *The Atlantic*."

But our desks were never meant to be our altars. The modern labor force evolved to serve the needs of consumers and capitalists, not to satisfy tens of millions of people seeking transcendence at the office. It's hard to self-actualize on the job if you're a cashier—one of the most common occupations in the US—and even the best white-collar roles have long periods of stasis, boredom, or busywork. This mismatch between expectations and reality is a recipe for severe disappointment, if not outright misery, and it might explain why rates of depression and anxiety in the US are "substantially higher" than they were in the 1980s, according to a 2014 study.

One of the benefits of being an observant Christian, Muslim, or Zoroastrian is that these God-fearing worshippers put their faith in an intangible and unfalsifiable force of goodness. But work is tangible, and success is often falsified. To make either the centerpiece of one's life is to place one's esteem in the mercurial hands of the market. To be a workist is to worship a god with firing power.

2. The Millennial Workist

The Millennial generation—born in the past two decades of the 20th century—came of age in the roaring 1990s, when workism coursed through the veins of American society. On the West Coast, the modern tech sector emerged, minting millionaires who combined utopian dreams with a do-what-you-love ethos. On the East Coast, President Clinton grabbed the neoliberal baton from Ronald Reagan and George H. W. Bush and signed laws that made work the nucleus of welfare policy.

As Anne Helen Petersen wrote in a viral essay on "Millennial burnout" for *BuzzFeed News*—building on ideas Malcolm Harris addressed in his book *Kids These Days*— Millennials were honed in these decades into machines of self-optimization. They passed through a childhood of extracurricular overachievement and checked every box of the success sequence, only to have the economy blow up their dreams.

While it's inadvisable to paint 85 million people with the same brush, it's fair to say that American Millennials have been collectively defined by two external traumas. The first is student debt. Millennials are the most educated generation ever, a distinction that should have made them rich and secure. But rising educational attainment has come at a steep price. Since 2007, outstanding student debt has grown by almost $1 trillion, roughly tripling in just 12 years. And since the economy cratered in 2008, average wages for young graduates have stagnated—making it even harder to pay off loans.

The second external trauma of the Millennial generation has been the disturbance of social media, which has amplified the pressure to craft an image of success—for oneself, for one's friends and colleagues, and even for one's parents. But literally visualizing career success can be difficult in a services and information economy. Blue-collar jobs produce tangible products, like coal, steel rods, and houses. The output of white-collar work—algorithms, consulting projects, programmatic advertising campaigns—is more shapeless and often quite invisible. It's not glib to say that the whiter the collar, the more invisible the product.

Since the physical world leaves few traces of achievement, today's workers turn to social media to make manifest their accomplishments. Many of them spend hours crafting a separate reality of stress-free smiles, post-card vistas, and Edison-lightbulbed working spaces. "The social media feed [is] evidence of the fruits of hard, rewarding labor and the labor itself," Petersen writes.

Among Millennial workers, it seems, overwork and "burnout" are outwardly celebrated (even if, one suspects, they're inwardly mourned). In a recent *New York Times* essay, "Why Are Young People Pretending to Love Work?," the reporter Erin Griffith pays a visit to the co-working space WeWork, where the pillows urge DO WHAT YOU LOVE, and the neon signs implore workers to HUSTLE HARDER. These dicta resonate with young workers. As several studies show, Millennials are meaning junkies at work. "Like all employees," one Gallup survey concluded, "millennials care about their income. But for this genera-tion, a job is about more than a paycheck, it's about a purpose."

The problem with this gospel—Your dream job is out there, so never stop hustling—is that it's a blueprint for spiritual and physical exhaustion. Long hours don't make anybody more productive or creative; they make people stressed, tired, and bitter. But the overwork myths survive "because they justify the extreme wealth created for a small group of elite techies," Griffith writes.

There is something slyly dystopian about an economic system that has convinced the most indebted generation in American history to put purpose over paycheck. Indeed, if you were designing a "Black Mirror" labor force that encouraged overwork without higher wages, what might you do? Perhaps you'd persuade educated young people that income comes second; that no job is just a job; and that the only real reward from work is the ineffable glow of purpose. It is a diabolical game that creates a prize so tantalizing yet rare that almost nobody wins, but everybody feels obligated to play forever.

3. Time for Happiness

This is the right time for a confession. I am the very thing that I am criticizing.

I am devoted to my job. I feel most myself when I am fulfilled by my work—including the work of writing an essay about work. My sense of identity is so bound up in my job, my sense of accomplishment, and my feeling of productivity that bouts of writer's block can send me into an existential funk that can spill over into every part of my life. And I know enough writers, tech workers, marketers, artists, and entrepreneurs to know that my affliction is common, especially within a certain tranche of the white-collar workforce.

Some workists, moreover, seem deeply fulfilled. These happy few tend to be intrinsically motivated; they don't need to share daily evidence of their accomplishments.

A

But maintaining the purity of internal motivations is harder in a world where social media and mass media are so adamant about externalizing all markers of success. There's *Forbes*'s list of this, and *Fortune*'s list of that; and every Twitter and Facebook and LinkedIn profile is conspicuously marked with the metrics of accomplishment—followers, friends, viewers, retweets—that inject all communication with the features of competition. It may be getting harder each year for purely motivated and sincerely happy workers to opt out of the tournament of labor swirling around them.

Workism offers a perilous trade-off. On the one hand, Americans' high regard for hard work may be responsible for its special place in world history and its reputation as the global capital of start-up success. A culture that worships the pursuit of extreme success will likely produce some of it. But extreme success is a falsifiable god, which rejects the vast majority of its worshippers. Our jobs were never meant to shoulder the burdens of a faith, and they are buckling under the weight. A staggering 87 percent of employees are not engaged at their job, according to Gallup. That number is rising by the year.

One solution to this epidemic of disengagement would be to make work less awful. But maybe the better prescription is to make work less central.

This can start with public policy. There is new enthusiasm for universal policies—like universal basic income, parental leave, subsidized child care, and a child allowance—which would make long working hours less necessary for all Americans. These changes alone might not be enough to reduce Americans' devotion to work for work's sake, since it's the rich who are most devoted. But they would spare the vast majority of the public from the pathological workaholism that grips today's elites, and perhaps create a bottom-up movement to displace work as the centerpiece of the secular American identity.

On a deeper level, Americans have forgotten an old-fashioned goal of working: It's about buying free time. The vast majority of workers are happier when they spend more hours with family, friends, and partners, according to research conducted by Ashley Whillans, an assistant professor at Harvard Business School. In one study, she concluded that the happiest young workers were those who said around the time of their college graduation that they preferred careers that gave them time away from the office to focus on their relationships and their hobbies.

How quaint that sounds. But it's the same perspective that inspired the economist John Maynard Keynes to predict in 1930 that Americans would eventually have five-day weekends, rather than five-day weeks. It is the belief—the faith, even—that work is not life's product, but its currency. What we choose to buy with it is the ultimate project of living.

A

WHAT IS THE OFFICE FOR?

September 2021

IN MARCH 2020, THE WORLD shut down. Like thousands of white-collar companies around the world, Microsoft told its employees to stay home. Months later, the company had not fallen apart. Quite the opposite. Its market valuation boomed to more than $2 trillion, and its earnings grew considerably. The company realized that the pandemic had tragically created the perfect opportunity to answer a deep, almost existential question: What is the office *for*?

To answer this question in a serious and scientific way, Microsoft researchers teamed up with the University of California Berkeley to conduct an experiment. They tracked the anonymized communications habits of 61,000 employees. They wanted to know how the pandemic and remote work changed the way that colleagues talked and collaborated.

In 2021, they published the results of their research, with a clear upshot: With remote work, the teams got deeper. But the walls between teams got higher.

Messages sent among team members went way up. Groups who were used to working together in the office were active at replacing those interactions with a barrage of messages and meetings. But remote work took a battering ram to what the researchers called "out-group connections." These relationships come in many forms. Maybe, before the pandemic, you occasionally got lunch with someone to swap stories about raising young daughters. Maybe, on the way to the bathroom, you often stopped by somebody's desk to talk about basketball. Or maybe you bumped into the person who sat next to you at your new-employee orientation and liked to talk crap about the company from time to time. Ties plummeted between teams, between loosely affiliated workers, and between people who barely interacted at all.

In September 2021, I read this paper and called up the authors. "I have a theory about your theory, and I want you to tell me if it's horribly wrong," I said. They agreed to participate. "I think your paper is really about hard work versus soft work," I said. They didn't know what I meant. Neither did I. I had just made up these terms, and they probably required a firm definition.

Imagine dividing the day's work into two: hard work and soft work. "Hard work" is what I am literally paid to do. It's reading, researching, calling people, transcribing conversations, and writing articles. For others, maybe managing employees, working in Excel or PowerPoint, or reading and writing a zillion emails might count as hard work. (This kind of hard work, I should note, doesn't have to be physically laborious.) If the pandemic remote-work experiment taught us anything, it's that white-collar employees can do hard work from home just about as well as they can do it in the office—and maybe even better, precisely because their colleagues aren't interrupting them.

But then there's soft work. Soft work is the vague middle space of weekday activity that isn't hard work but also isn't *not-work*. Soft work is getting coffee with a co-worker. It's catching up about the NFL on Monday morning. If networking, schmoozing, gossiping, and mildly annoying people on your floor with "Hey, does this idea suck?" are species of behavior, soft work is the genus that contains them.

The Microsoft paper showed that the pandemic gutted the office and, in the process, destroyed a lot of soft work. That's because offices aren't for hard work. *Offices are for soft work.* The researchers listened patiently to my theory. They said I might be onto something.

SO THE TRILLION-DOLLAR QUESTION is: Who cares?

For a decade or more, productivity experts have been telling us that cross-group collaboration and weak ties are the skeleton key to unlocking radical creativity. In the abstract, this seems plausible. The history of invention is, in large part, a history of smart people making great leaps forward by combining disparate ideas in domains adjacent to their expertise. Since anything can be related to anything, we ought to build systems that allow people to see previously undiscovered connections between siloed domains.

Communicating across domains requires trust. And trust is hard earned among strangers. Several years ago, Google conducted a research project on its most productive groups. The company found that the most important quality was something called "psychological safety"—a confidence that team members wouldn't embarrass or punish individuals for speaking up. But there is something special about learning to trust people that you can physically see. By contrast, online communications can be a minefield for psychological safety. If you hand your boss a project, and they say "okay" in a kind and anticipatory way, you might be satisfied that they look forward to reviewing your work. If you email the same project to your boss, and they respond with a two-letter email— "ok"—you might jump to catastrophic conclusions about their opinion of your work. ("Just 'ok'!?") We get more data from people when we see their faces and gesticulations. Soft work—office banter, random gossip, and bad jokes—don't increase productivity in the short term, But over time, they can be the carrier wave for psychological safety and an amplifier for cross-team creativity.

But we shouldn't assume that offices are the only work arrangement that makes soft work possible. Perhaps in a

A

few decades, we'll realize that offices were terrible environments for building trust. Perhaps we'll learn that frequent team dinners, reunions, or retreats are a much better way to encourage colleagues to trust each other.

The loudest defenders of the office are defending a status quo that might not deserve so strong a defense. Here's a thought experiment. Imagine an alternate reality in which no such thing as an office existed in the 1900s and early 2000s. Until 2019, everybody worked remotely—in their homes, coffee shops, and libraries.

Then, in 2020, a strange virus broke out. It was transmitted by *aloneness*. Suddenly workers who had been happily (and sometimes not-so-happily) remote for decades were forced to cluster in large, open indoor spaces with adjacent desks called "cubicles." Physical rooms were built and reserved for what used to be Zoom calls but were then rebranded as "meetings." Gossip on Slack and IM was abruptly funneled into hallways. We called our newly synchronous chitchat "watercooler gossip," although this was an odd coinage as watercoolers were rarely visible on the premises. In short, for the first time in a century, white-collar Americans were forced to work in one another's physical proximity, and they discovered, to their horror and delight, that the proportion of soft work in their day had dramatically expanded. Some people, especially extroverts and some managers, welcomed this change. Spending their weekdays just, like, talking to corporeal beings all the time was such a pleasure! Others hated the new arrangement so much they promptly quit.

The point of this hypothetical is twofold. First, inverting reality sometimes helps show that even the most familiar institutions are also inventions. Second, in a very real way, it's not a hypothetical. Remote is still the status quo for many American workers now. People are quitting their jobs rather than be forced back into offices. It is the corporate headquarters, not the bedroom office, that is, or is about to be, the novel intrusion for much of today's white-collar workforce.

The lesson of the Microsoft study is that offices seem to be excellent at a specific job: They increase soft work across silos. But rather than think of toiling in offices as the good, normal thing to which we'll inevitably return, we should think of it as one of many working arrangements that deserve our scrutiny and skepticism.

A

THE BIGGEST PROBLEM
WITH REMOTE WORK

July 2022

REMOTE WORK SEEMS FULLY ENTRENCHED in American life. Offices are more than half empty nationwide, while restaurants and movie theaters are packed. Housing prices in suburbs and small towns have surged as white-collar workers take advantage of the demise of the daily commute.

But if the work-from-anywhere movement has been successful for veteran employees in defined roles with trusted colleagues, for certain people and for certain objectives, remote or hybrid work remains a problem to be solved.

First, remote work is worse for *new workers*. Many inexperienced employees joining a virtual company realize that they haven't joined much of a company at all. They've logged into a virtual room that calls itself a company but is basically a group chat. It's hard to promote a wholesome company culture in normal times, and harder still to do so one misunderstood group Slack message and problematic fire emoji at a time. "Small talk, passing conversations, even just observing your manager's pathways through the office may seem trivial, but in the aggregate they're far more valuable than any form of company handbook," write Anne Helen Petersen and Charlie Warzel, the authors of the book *Out of Office*. Many of the perks of flexible work—like owning your own schedule and getting away from office gossip—can "work against younger employees" in companies that don't have intentional structured mentorship programs, they argued.

Second, remote is worse at building *new teams* to take on new tasks. In 2020, Microsoft tapped researchers from UC Berkeley to study how the pandemic changed its work culture. Researchers combed through 60,000 employees' anonymized messages and chats. They found that the number of messages sent within teams grew significantly, as workers tried to keep up with their colleagues. But information sharing between groups plummeted. Remote work made people more likely to hunker down with their preexisting teams and less likely to have serendipitous conversations that could lead to knowledge sharing. Though employees could accomplish the "hard work" of emailing and making PowerPoints from anywhere, the Microsoft-Berkeley study suggested that the most important job of the office is "soft work"—the sort of banter that allows for long-term trust and innovation.

Other major studies have come to similar conclusions. In 2022, researchers from MIT and UCLA published a map of face-to-face interactions in the Bay Area made using smartphone geolocation data and matched it to patent citations by individual firms. They were looking for empirical evidence to support the old Jane Jacobs theory that cities promote innovation as people from disparate walks of life bump into each other and cross-pollinate ideas. They concluded that the Jacobs theory was right. The groups and firms with the most face-to-face interactions also had the most unique patent citations.

Third, and relatedly, remote work is worse at generating disruptive *new ideas*. A paper published in *Nature* by Melanie Brucks, at Columbia Business School, and Jonathan Levav, at the Stanford Graduate School of Business, analyzed whether virtual teams could brainstorm as creatively as in-person teams. In one study, they recruited about 1,500 engineers to work in pairs and randomly assigned them to brainstorm either face-to-face or over videoconference. After the pairs generated product ideas for an hour, they selected and submitted one to a panel of judges. Engineers who worked virtually generated fewer total ideas and external raters graded their ideas significantly less creative than those of the in-person teams.

The Stanford economist Nicholas Bloom—a famous defender of remote work's potential—told me that this study presented the "best research" on how in-person interactions foster complex, free-flowing discussion. "There are definitely situations, including mentoring new employees and innovative activities, that require some time in the office," he said. "For me, that does not mean that [work from home] is bad, but that it cannot be 100 percent of work."

Why might the quality of ideas degrade when people collaborate remotely? My favorite explanation is that collaboration requires trust, and trust implies a kind of intimacy, and it's hard to build true intimacy via Zoom and chat. One of the most profound things that I've heard in my two years reporting on remote work is the idea that digital communications can be a minefield for trust.

"Whenever we read a sentence on Gchat or Slack that seems ambiguous or sarcastic to us, we default to thinking, *You fucker!*" Bill Duane, a remote-work consultant and former Google engineer, told me. "But if someone had said the same thing to your face, you might be laughing with them." In many contexts, remote work without physical-world reunions can flatten colleagues into simplistic caricatures and abstractions. It sounds hokey but it's true: To see our colleagues as whole people, we have to literally see them *as whole people*—not just two-dimensional avatars.

The work-from-anywhere revolution has something of a kick-starter problem: It's harder for new workers, new groups, and new ideas to get revved up.

So how do we fix this? One school of thought says face-to-face interactions are too precious to be replaced. I disagree. I'm an optimist who believes the corporate world

A

can solve these problems, because I know that other industries already have.

Modern scientific research is a team sport, with groups spanning many universities and countries. Groups working without face-to-face interaction have historically been less innovative, according to a new paper on remote work in science. For decades, teams split among several countries were *five times* less likely to produce "breakthrough" science that replaced the corpus of research that came before it. But in the past decade, the innovation gap between on-site and remote teams suddenly reversed. Today, the teams divided by the greatest distance are producing the most significant and innovative work.

I asked one of the co-authors of the paper, the Oxford University economist Carl Benedikt Frey, to explain this flip. He said the explosion of remote-work tools such as Zoom and Slack was essential. But the most important factor is that remote scientists have figured out how to be better hybrid workers. After decades of trial and error, they've learned to combine their local networks, which are developed through years of in-person encounters, and their virtual networks, to build a kind of global collective brain.

If scientists can make remote work work, companies can do it too. But they might just have to create an entirely new position—a middle manager for the post-pandemic era.

IN THE MIDDLE OF the 19th century, the railroads and the telegraph allowed goods and information to move faster than ever. In 1800, traveling from Manhattan to Chicago took, on average, four weeks. In 1857, it took two days. Firms headquartered in major cities could suddenly track prices from Los Angeles to Miami and ship goods across the country at then-record-high speeds.

To conduct this full orchestra of operations, mid-1800s companies had to invent an entirely new system of organizing work. They needed a new layer of decision makers who could steer local production and distribution businesses. A new species of employee was born: the "middle manager."

"As late as 1840, there were no middle managers in the United States," Alfred Chandler observed in *The Visible Hand*, his classic history of the rise of America's managerial revolution. In the early 1800s, all managers were owners, and all owners were managers; it was unheard of for somebody to direct employees without being a partner in the company. But once ownership and management were unbundled, new kinds of American companies were made possible, such as the department store, the mail-order house, and the national oil and steel behemoths.

In the 1800s, new technology allowed US companies to extend their distribution and production tentacles across the continent, necessitating a new class of worker.

Today's hybrid companies, similarly extended across the country and even around the world, need to invent a new role to remain competitive and sane. This role would determine what work was "hard work" that could be done asynchronously and from anywhere, and what necessary "soft work" would require people to be in an office at the same time. Based on a comprehensive understanding of total workflow and team dynamics, this person would develop and constantly update a plan of who needs to be in the office, and on what days, and where they sit, and *why they are there in the first place.*

Operations teams at many companies are already doing some of this work. Often these teams are spread across multiple challenges that preexisted the pandemic— like recruiting, IT, office maintenance, and normal pre-pandemic communications. For these stressed and over-stretched workers, coordinating the perfect hybrid cadence is the third priority for five different people. But managing a remote or hybrid workflow is too important to sprinkle onto old positions. It's a discrete task, with discrete challenges, which deserves a discrete job.

The synchronizer—or, for large companies, a team of synchronizers—would be responsible for solving the new-worker, new-group, and new-idea problems. Synchronizers would help new workers by ensuring that their managers, mentors, and colleagues are with them at the office during an early onboarding period. They would plan in-person time for new teammates to get to know one another as actual people and not just abstracted online personalities. They would coordinate the formation of new groups to tackle new project ideas, the same way that modern teams in science pull together the right researchers from around the world to co-author new papers. They would plan frequent retreats and reunions across the company, even for workers who never have to be together, with the understanding that the best new ideas—whether in science, consulting, or media—often come from the surprising hybridization of disparate expertise.

The remote-work debate has become deeply polarized between people who consider it a moral necessity that is beyond criticism and those who consider it a culture-killer that is beyond fixing. Like the office, remote work will never go away, and like the office, it has important problems that deserve our attention. Solving remote work's problems is a job worth doing.

A

WHY WE HAVE NO TIME

———————

December 2019

ONE OF THE TRUISMS OF modern life is that nobody has any time. Everybody is busy, burned out, swamped, *overwhelmed*. So let's try a simple thought experiment. Imagine that you came into possession of a magical new set of technologies that could automate or expedite every single part of your job.

What would you do with the extra time? Maybe you'd pick up a hobby, or have more children, or learn to luxuriate in the additional leisure. But what if I told you that you wouldn't do any of those things: You would just work the *exact same amount of time as before.*

I can't prove this, because I don't know you. What I do know is that something remarkably similar to my hypothetical happened in the US economy in the 20th century—not in factories, or in modern offices. But inside American homes.

The household economy of cooking, cleaning, mending, washing, and grocery shopping has arguably changed more in the past 100 years than the American factory or the modern office. And its evolution tells an illuminating story about why, no matter what work we do, we never seem to have enough time. In the 20th century, labor-saving household technology improved dramatically, but no labor appears to have been saved.

Technologically, the typical American home of 1900 wasn't so different from the typical home of 1500. Bereft of modern equipment, it had no electricity. Although some rich families had indoor plumbing, most did not. Family members were responsible for ferrying each drop of water in and out of the house.

The following decades brought a bevy of labor-saving appliances. Air conditioning and modern toilets, for starters. But also refrigerators and freezers, electric irons, vacuum cleaners, and dishwashers.

These machines worked miracles. Electric stoves made food prep faster. Automatic washers and dryers cut the time needed to clean a load of clothes. Refrigerators meant that housewives and the help didn't have to worry about buying fresh food every other day.

Each of these innovations could have saved hours of labor. But none of them did. At first, these new machines compensated for the decline in home servants. (They helped cause that decline, as well.) Then housework expanded to fill the available hours. In 1920, full-time housewives spent 51 hours a week on housework, according to Juliet Schor, an economist and the author of *The*

A

Overworked American. In the 1950s, they worked 52 hours a week. In the 1960s, they worked 53 hours. Half a century of labor-saving technology does not appear to have saved the typical housewife even one minute of labor.

This might seem impossible. But there are three simple reasons for this—and each has clear implications for why a combination of individual psychology and structural forces makes it so hard for Americans to find more time, even in an economy that is becoming ever more rich and technologically sophisticated.

1. Better technology means higher expectations— and higher expectations create more work.

For most of history, humans blithely languished in their own filth. Most families' clothes were washed on a semi-annual basis, and body odor was inescapable. The fleet of housework technologies that sprang into the world between the late-19th and mid-20th century created new norms of cleanliness—for our floors, our clothes, *ourselves*.

New norms meant more work. Automatic washers and dryers raised our expectations for clean clothes and encouraged people to go out and buy new shirts and pants; housewives therefore had more loads of laundry to wash, dry, and fold. As one 1920s housewife wrote, of her new dusting and mopping and furniture-polish technology, "Because we housewives of today have the tools to reach it, we dig every day after dust that grandmother left to a spring cataclysm."

New home tech also created new kinds of work that absorbed the extra time. For example, refrigerators made it easier to keep food fresh and electric ovens made it faster to cook. But housewives used this convenience to spend more time driving to the supermarket to buy fresh produce to stock the fridge. Between the 1920s and the 1960s, Schor writes, time spent prepping food fell by about 10 hours a week. But time spent shopping for food increased, in part thanks to another 20th-century invention: the supermarket.

In short, technology made it much easier to clean a house to 1890s standards. But by mid-century, Americans didn't want that old house. They wanted a modern home—with delicious meals and dustless windowsills and glistening floors—and this delicious and dustless glisten required a 40-to-50-hour workweek, even with the assistance of modern tools.

In the 1950s, a British civil servant coined the term *Parkinson's Law* to explain the phenomenon that "work expands to fill the available time." The rule first described the seemingly infinite busywork of government bureaucracies. But it might also apply to housework. Expectations rose, and work expanded to fill the available time.

This story offers one explanation for why leisure hasn't much increased for many rich workers in the 21st century. We'd collectively prefer more money and more *stuff* rather than more downtime. We are victims of the curse of want.

2. A lot of modern overwork is class and status maintenance—for this generation and the next.

As technology has reduced the time it takes to cook a meal or wash a shirt, it's opened up more hours in the day to care for other parts of the house. Such as the little humans living in it.

In the past few decades, child care has been the fastest growing component of housework. Since the 1980s, American parents—and particularly college-educated mothers and fathers—have nearly doubled the amount of time they spend raising, teaching, driving, and helping their kids. The economist Valerie Ramey chalks it up to a "rug rat race" led by middle- and upper-class parents devoting more hours to prepare their kids for competitive college admissions and a cutthroat labor force.

Ramey sees the rug rat race as, in part, an anxious status- and income-maintenance ritual for the college-educated class. "When my husband [the economist Gary Ramey] and I first looked at this, the research was semi-autobiographical, because we couldn't believe the amount of pressure our friends were putting on their kids to get ready for college," she told me. "In the old regime, college-educated parents could get their kids into good schools because the marginal slot was being filled by a first-generation college student," she said. But today, far more children of college-educated parents are competing for a finite number of seats.

Many young people concerned with burnout don't have kids. But their motivations are an extension of the same impulse behind concerted parenting—they, too, feel like participants in a pseudo-meritocratic rat race, and they're terrified of losing status, class, or future income. Young YouTube stars work to exhaustion to meet the expectations of an algorithm that prizes daily content. Lawyers and consultants work overtime to prove to their bosses that they will sacrifice every shred of their personal life to help their firms crush global rivals. Some of these rat-race participants might truly be on the brink of financial emergency. But a lot of them are yuppie workists who have made a secular religion out of the pursuit of status and professional fulfillment. Like Valerie Ramey's friends, their overwork isn't so much about avoiding poverty as it is about avoiding the psychically difficult prospect that life, in this generation and the next, isn't an infinite escalator.

These first two explanations might be compelling, but they're also incomplete. They both imply that housework

A

and modern work are things that workers have total agency over, when, in fact, most people's working lives are not entirely theirs to control.

3. Technology only frees people from work if the boss—or the government, or the economic system—allows it.

Many stay-at-home moms, today and throughout the last century, have been happy to play their crucial role in the family economy. But one thing that Schor emphasizes is that underinvestment in women, and low expectations about their potential in the labor force, have played a big role in forcing many would-be woman employees to stay out of the workforce.

"I think the biggest reason that labor-saving technology in the home didn't actually reduce labor for housewives is that the opportunity cost of women's labor was socially valued at zero," Schor told me. "By that I mean, a lot of men wanted their wives to keep busy but assumed that they would be worthless outside the home, as salaried workers, like lawyers or doctors." Many women were caught between the husband's expectation that they be useful and a male-dominated society that blocked them from education and salaried labor. As a result, they had little choice but to spend their full 40- to 50-hour workweek preparing the home for the family.

Housework hours finally fell only when women joined the labor force en masse. Since the 1960s, the share of women in the workforce has increased by about 50 percent. In that time, the typical adult woman has decreased her housework hours by about one-third, according to analysis by the economist Valerie Ramey. That is, the one thing that finally reduced labor *in* the home was . . . labor *outside* of the home.

What does this history tell us about life in the 21st century? Bosses set hours and income, and workers adjust. When husbands controlled their wives' schedules, they insisted on a clean and tidy home and a ready-made dinner; and their wives typically obliged. When today's employers hire a full-time worker under modern labor laws, they insist on a 40-hour week, or more; and the worker typically obliges. It doesn't matter whether technology stays the same, or improves by leaps and bounds. The workweek is fixed and predetermined. A meaningful, economy-wide reduction in work hours would likely require changing the laws that determine the relationship between employers and employees.

4. Leisure is getting "leaky."

Here is a final theory that applies equally to all income brackets: Thanks to smartphones and computers, leisure activity is leaking into work, and work, too, is leaking into

A

leisure. As a result, more workers—and white-collar workers, especially—are still at work, even long after the workday is over.

Technology makes content leaky. The radio set used to be a living room fixture. To listen to the radio, it was necessary to be at home. Then the car radio liberated the radio from the living room, and the television set replaced its corner of the living room. Then the smartphone liberated video from the television screen and put it on a mobile device that fit in people's pockets.

Now somebody can listen to music, watch video, and read—while checking on social media feeds that can act as the cumulative equivalent of newspapers, magazines, and phone calls with friends—on their phone, while at work. Meanwhile, these same mobile instruments of leisure are also instruments of professional connectivity: When a boss knows that each of her workers has a smartphone, she knows that they can all read her email on a Saturday morning (sent, naturally, at 4:01 a.m.).

My job fits snugly into this category. Writing is a leaky affair, where the boundaries between work and leisure are always porous. When I open Twitter, or watch the news on a Sunday morning, am I panning for golden nuggets of insight, taking a mental-health break, or something in between? It's difficult to say; sometimes, I don't even know. A novel that I read can become an article's lede. A history book on my desk can inspire a column. Because the scope of nonfiction journalism is boundless, every moment of my downtime could theoretically surface an idea or stray comment that becomes a story. As a result, my weekdays feel more like weekends; and my weekends feel more like weekdays.

Let's return to the original question: *Why don't Americans have more free time?* In my experience, the debate over labor and leisure is often fought between the Self-Helpers and the Socialists. The Self-Helpers say that individuals have agency to solve their problems and can reduce their anxiety through new habits and values. The Socialists say that this individualist ethos is a dangerous myth. Instead, they insist that almost all modern anxieties arise from structural inequalities that require structural solutions, like a dramatic reconfiguration of the economy and stronger labor laws to protect worker rights.

The history of American housework suggests that both sides have a point. Americans tend to use new productivity and technology to buy a better life rather than to enjoy more downtime in inferior conditions. And when material concerns are mostly met, Americans fixate on their status and class, and that of their children, and work tirelessly to preserve and grow it.

But most Americans don't have the economic or political power to negotiate a better deal for themselves. Their working hours and income are shaped by higher powers, like bosses, federal laws, and societal expectations.

A

To solve the problems of overwork and time starvation, we have to recognize both that individuals have the agency to make small changes to improve their lives and that, without broader changes to our laws and norms and social expectations, no amount of overwork will ever be enough.

TIME AND CAPITALISM

December 2016

WHAT IS AN ECONOMY? You might say it is how people who cannot predict the future deal with it.

People save money to protect themselves from calamity. Banks charge interest to account for risk. People trade stocks to bet on the earnings trajectory of a company. The first taxes were levied to support standing armies that could fight in the event of an invasion.

Time's unknowable perils contributed to the flourishing of economic thought. But then something interesting happened. The creature became the creator: The economy re-invented time. Or, to put things less obliquely, the age of exploration and the industrial revolution completely changed the way people measure time, understand time, and feel and talk about time.

Just think: What do you look forward to when you're at work? Maybe it's a happy hour, the weekend, or, in the more distant future, retirement. Each of these are distinct periods of time, and each is an invention of the last 150 years of economic change.

The word _weekend_ is a creation of the industrial revolution, since a discrete working week doesn't make much

A

sense on a farm that needs constant tending. *Retirement*, as a term, dates back to the 1600s, as it relates to army service, but its modern usage only became mainstream after the move to an industrial economy. *Happy hour* is a neologism from the 1950s, a heyday for workplace optimism. The equally hopeful *T.G.I.F* acronym comes from the post–World War II era.

Three forces contributed to the modern invention of time. First, the conquest of foreign territories across the ocean required precise navigation with accurate timepieces. Second, the invention of the railroad required the standardization of time across countries, replacing the local system of keeping time using shadows and sundials. Third, the industrial economy necessitated new labor laws, which changed the way people think about work.

1. The Emperor's New Clocks

The history of timepieces is a history of empires.

Long before the modern clock used springs and familiar markings, just about every great civilization had attempted to measure time, with each one failing in its own special way. In ancient Egypt, China, and Mesopotamia, sundials, or "shadow clocks," all required bright sunlight to count the hours, which wasn't of much use on overcast days. To work around this problem, some of these ancient civilizations used a "water clock," or clepsydra, a device that steadily dripped water through a small hole into a container with lines painted around the side to represent the passage of time. But slight changes in temperature could change the viscosity of water and the rate of drips. On a cold day, the water might freeze, and so would time.

The most important breakthroughs in the history of horology required the incentives and resources of a global empire. Toward the end of the Exploration Age, the great powers like England, France, and Spain struggled to navigate the oceans, because they couldn't accurately measure longitude, or their progress east or west of their site of departure. As a result, they would crash into rocks or get lost and run out of food.

To some, this seemed like a problem of orientation. To John Harrison, an English carpenter, it was clearly a problem of time. Imagine that a ship departs from London for Jamaica with two clocks. The first clock keeps perfect London time throughout the journey. The second clock is reset to noon each day on the ocean when the sun reaches its highest point in the sky. As a result, the time difference between the two clocks grows as the ship sails toward the Americas. As you know, the earth rotates 360 degrees every 24 hours. That means 15 degrees every hour. So, for each hour that the two clocks were apart, the ship had traveled 15 degrees west—or about 900 nautical miles,

A

which is roughly the distance between New York City and Missouri; a time zone.

The scenario above isn't a hypothetical; it's precisely the calculation that Harrison made. The subject of the classic book *Longitude* by Dava Sobel, Harrison became famous for building the two most advanced clocks (technically: chronometers) of all time. His timepieces didn't rely on the dripping of water, flow of sand, or even the swinging of heavy pendula. They were precise and durable enough to withstand the ricketty journey across the ocean. For his pains—he spent about 30 years designing and tweaking the timepieces—he won a luxurious prize from the British government.

The British Empire didn't merely help perfect the modern timepiece but also helped to popularize the watch. In the late 1800s, watches were considered to be feminine jewelry; men kept their timepieces tucked away in pockets. But in colonial campaigns like the First Boer War and the Third Burmese War, British commanders tied little clocks to their soldiers' wrists. Going into battle with feminine jewelry might have struck the men of war as uniform malfunction. But the innovation proved extremely useful for coordinating troop movements.

By World War I, watches were standard-issue gear for soldiers in the trenches. When the men who survived came home, they retained the habit. Thus the wristwatch, conceived as a piece of jewelry for women, was re-marketed through colonial warfare as a thoroughly masculine fashion. By the 1930s, wristwatches were the norm and the pocket watch was an anachronism. Time, itself, had become a human appendage.

2. Time-Zone Travel

Time and space are connected, not only in the fabric of the universe, but also in our idioms. We talk about time as an interval applying both to moments ("It's fifteen minutes to five") and to geography ("I'm fifteen minutes from Five Guys"). Perhaps this is why the invention of a machine to zoom through space, the train, inspired the idea that a machine might travel through time.

The rise of the railroad in the 1800s startled the era's scientists and inspired a new ecstatic language of progress. In 1864's *Journey to the Center of the Earth*, Jules Verne imagined a machine that, rather than navigate the circumference of the earth, departed along the perpendicular axis to travel inward through the mantle of its sphere. In 1895's *The Time Machine*, H. G. Wells's protagonist embarks along another dimension, time, as if history itself were a navigable rail line stretching from past to future. Humans had been trying to predict the future since before the Oracle of Delphi. Only after the invention of trains did they imagine visiting it.

A

The discovery of machine-power was, in many ways, the discovery of the future. "Travelers riding in steam-driven railroad trains looked out their windows onto a landscape where oxen plowed the fields as they had done in medieval times, horses still hauled and harrowed, yet telegraph wires split the sky," James Gleick writes in *Time Travel*, his wondrous interdisciplinary history of the subject. (Those interested in a simpler history of time might also enjoy the delightful young adult book *This Book Is About Time*.) "This caused a new kind of confusion or dissociation," Gleick wrote. "Call it temporal dissonance."

Dissonance is right. The railroad created a crisis of time management unlike anything human beings had ever experienced. In the pre-train age, all time was local, divined mostly by the angle of the sun in the sky. If Philadelphia and Harrisburg had different times, nobody noticed, because a Philly resident couldn't reach Harrisburg by phone or rail to tell the difference. As a result there were hundreds of local times in the United States.

Local time was perfectly suitable for a local agrarian economy. But for a railroad company and its customers, it was a nightmare. Imagine walking through an airport terminal (already logistical chaos) and learning that Delta and United now operate by entirely separate time schedules: A United flight that takes off, on-time, at 1 p.m. leaves at the same time as a Delta flight departing on-time at

2 p.m., and the clocks on the wall correspond to neither Delta nor United.

That sounds ludicrous. But for the first railroad travelers, this scenario was commonplace. In Buffalo's train station, each railroad company used its own time schedule. The New York Central Railroad ran on New York time. The Michigan Southern Railroad schedule ran on the local time of Columbus, Ohio. And both of those clocks were distinct from the clock that represented local Buffalo time.

As Gleick writes, "Railroads made time zones inevitable." The railroad companies finally got together in the 1880s and decided to divide the US into four standard time zones: eastern, central, mountain, pacific. This required local communities to forfeit their control of time, which didn't go over well in a country founded on federalist principles. To many, the standardization of time seemed like a national takeover. Others accused jewelers of orchestrating the time-zone revolution to make people buy new clocks and watches.

The four zones were set on November 18, 1883. The precise times were dictated by another new technology that seemed to pierce the boundary of space and time, the telegraph. The following year, the International Time Conference established the plan for global time zones, which included an International Date Line. And so, wristwatches and standard time—perhaps the two most famous icons of horology—were both children of travel.

A

Nobody complains much about time zones anymore, unless they're whining about jet lag. Instead, we reserve our hate for Daylight Saving Time (DST). Initially instituted by Germany to save fuel during World War I, DST was first proposed in the US during the same war. Contrary to the popular idea that daylight saving time was a carrot to farmers, it was urban retailers looking to save artificial light costs who were among the staunchest advocates. Farmers actually led a national effort to repeal national daylight saving time in 1919. Yearlong DST returned in 1942, when President Franklin D. Roosevelt instituted "War Time," two months after Pearl Harbor, and only returned to normal standard time in 1945. Time waits for no man, but when a nation is at war, it gets pushed around quite a bit.

Beyond standard time, the subtler impact of railroads was their invention of the 21st-century concept of a career. The word itself comes from the French *carriere*, meaning a racetrack. To achieve its modern meaning, however, work required an element of vocational progress. Farm workers reached peak earnings as early as their 20s. But it took decades for railroad employees to earn their highest wages even in the late-1800s, as late as their 40s.

As the economy shifted from plows to rails, it changed the shape of one's lifetime earnings. Rather than a wage progression resembling a great plain—a flat, unchanging (or, perhaps, unpredictable) salary for many decades—the industrial revolution delivered the familiar curve of income that modern workers recognize, with gradually rising wages until middle-age, followed by a slow decline. And so, the industrial economy invented the very concept of a modern career, making the passage of time a materially significant matter for turn-of-the-century workers. (In fact, even the term "turn of the century" was only invented at the dawn of the 20th; before that, presumably, the centuries faded, like the shadow of sundials, or ran dry, like water clocks.)

3. Working for the Weekend

"What's your schedule like?"

It is one of the most common questions imaginable in a modern workplace. But if you asked somebody in the 1400s or 1700s, she would have no idea what you were talking about. The English word *schedule* dates back to the middle ages, when for hundreds of years it merely signified a slip of paper. But the modern definition—an orderly sequence of events and times—is a far more recent invention, coming from the late 1800s. The word first applied to a railroad company's list of train departures. (As does the word commute, derived from a "commutation ticket" or a season pass to a streetcar or railroad.)

For the next half century, American industrialists became obsessed with optimizing, well, schedules. If

A

the late 19th century turned time into a cultural fasci-
nation, the 20th century turned it into an economic
denominator.

The 1910s saw Henry Ford's Model-T assembly line
and Frederick Winslow Taylor's *The Principles of Scientific
Management*. Taylor's productivity treatise divided labor
into discrete activities—open the mail, hammer the
nail—and encouraged maximizing production over time
(while often minimizing wages over time). The first use of
time clocks to mark workers' hours of arrival grew in tan-
dem with Taylor's scientific management theories. Once a
tool of military coordination, watches had become keep-
ers of factory efficiency. Even their manufacturers adver-
tised time-clocks as tools for a "profitable" employee.

As for the workers, the long history of the US labor
movement has been in many ways an attempt to move
from an open-ended commitment to work as long as
possible to a legal framework to limit the workday and
workweek—a protest to reclaim time. Some of the first
American labor protests called for a 10-hour work day,
something today's workers would consider horrific.

But they had to start somewhere, since it wasn't
uncommon for early-1800s textile employees to work 12
hours daily. In 1840, Martin Van Buren signed an executive order for a 10-hour day. By the 1860s, the Grand
Eight Hours Leagues and the Knights of Labor were
pushing to shave another two hours off the workweek. In

1868, President Ulysses S. Grant signed a proclamation instituting an eight-hour work day for government employees. It was extended to railroad workers in 1915 and then to the entire private sector under the Fair Labor Standards Act of 1937. Soon the labor movement's attention turned from the workday to the workweek, advocating for a two-day weekend. Between 1920 and 1927 the number of large companies with official five-day workweeks increased by a factor of eight.

All told, in the last century and a half, the workweek has shrunk from 10 hours a day, six days a week, in the 1880s, to eight hours a day, five days a week—a 33 percent reduction. Where did the extra time go? Much went to leisure. The whole mountain of media that has grown in the last century—including weekly magazines, movies, radio, television, cable, and social media—relies on a resource, mass attention, that became abundant only as work declined as a share of the week.

4. The House of Time

The quantum physicists say that past and future are illusions. They say time is more like space. It's something that merely exists rather than unfolds. Imagine a house. All of the rooms are simply there, and it is an illusion that one room comes "after" or "before" another room. Instead, each individual's consciousness passing through the house

A

creates the illusion that there is an inviolable sequence of rooms.

The quantum theory of time would seem to have nothing to do with our economic history of horology. *Some scientists say time doesn't technically exist?* you might think. *Who cares, it sure as heck exists for me!* Normal people experience time as a flow, an infinite cascade of falling dominos, a chain of cause-and-effect events that neither leaps forward several moments nor suddenly reverses, but rather passes with the predictable click-click-click of now moments falling into the next with a steady cadence.

The purpose of an economy is to manage the perils of the future, to make sense of time, to make it work for *us*. In the 1930s, the economist John Maynard Keynes predicted that future economic productivity would reduce the long workweek to just 15 hours. So it's ironic that after several millennia of economic thought and evolution, some of the richest Americans haven't used their wealth to buy downtime. They've used it to buy more work. The richest Americans now work longer hours than they did a few decades ago.

As I've written, rich American men, in particular, are the world's chief workaholics, putting in longer hours than both rich people overseas and lower-income Americans. It's hard to say why. Perhaps mobile phones are an unbreakable leash. Perhaps the hunt for status and wealth among the plutocracy is yet another tether. Or perhaps rich people just love working ("building wealth to them is a creative process, and the closest thing they have to fun," as the economist Robert Frank wrote).

A recent study suggests that many of these workaholics have their values perfectly backward. Al E. Hershfield and Cassie Mogilner Holmes, assistant professors at the Anderson School of Management at UCLA, asked 4,000 Americans of various ages, income, jobs, and marital status: Would you take the money or the time? About two-thirds of their respondents said they'd take the money.

But those who valued time over money were happier, even when the researchers controlled for income. Among people with similarly high income, those most satisfied with life were far more likely to choose time. As they wrote, "The value individuals place on these resources relative to each other is predictive of happiness."

So much of what we now call time is a collective myth, devised by emperors, industrialists, protesters, and tinkerers. It's ironic, then, that the happiest workers are those who labor to buy time rather than money. The workaholics serve an illusive god. Then again, as the quantum physicists would say, so do we all.

A

ARTICLE CREDITS

ABOUT THE AUTHOR

DEREK THOMPSON is a staff writer at *The Atlantic*, where he publishes the newsletter "Work in Progress" on science, tech, and culture. He is the founder and host of the popular news podcast *Plain English with Derek Thompson*. A news analyst with NPR, Derek appears weekly on the national news show *Here and Now* and is also a contributor to CBS News. His first book, the national bestseller *Hit Makers: How to Succeed in an Age of Distraction*, has been translated into more than a dozen languages and was named the 2018 Book of the Year by the American Marketing Association. Derek lives in Washington, DC, with his wife and dog.